THE ERIE CANAL
A PRIMARY SOURCE HISTORY OF THE CANAL THAT CHANGED AMERICA

JANEY LEVY

rosen central
Primary Source

To my parents

Published in 2003 by The Rosen Publishing Group, Inc.
29 East 21st Street, New York, NY 10010

Library of Congress Cataloging-in-Publication Data

Levy, Janey.
The Erie Canal: a primary source history of the canal that changed America/ by Janey Levy.
  p. cm. — (Primary sources in American history)
Summary: Uses primary source documents, narrative, and illustrations to recount how construction of the Erie Canal changed America by vastly improving the movement of goods to settlers in the newly purchased Louisiana Territory.
Includes bibliographical references (p.) and index.
ISBN 0-8239-3680-5 (lib. bdg.)
1. Erie Canal (N.Y.)—History—Sources—Juvenile literature. [1. Erie Canal (N.Y.)—History—Sources. 2. Transportation—History—Sources. 3. New York (State)—History—Sources. 4. United States—History—19th century—Sources.]
I. Title. II. Series.
F127.E5 L48 2003
974.7—dc21

                                                                2002005608

Manufactured in the United States of America

CONTENTS

NTRODUCTION

It may be hard for people to imagine how difficult travel was at the beginning of the nineteenth century. Today, cars and interstate highways make travel fast and easy. However, in the early nineteenth century, travel was difficult and it took a long time. If you wanted to take a trip, you had to ride a horse or go in a carriage. Letters had to be carried to other towns by someone on horseback. Manufactured goods and agricultural products were transported by wagon. Roads were not good. There were thick forests to ride through and mountains to climb. The Appalachian Mountains, which cut through central New York, were so hard to cross that early Americans called them the "Endless Mountains."

AN IDEA IS BORN

In 1803, the United States bought the Louisiana Territory from France, and America became twice as large. This made improving transportation even more important. If settlers were going to move into this new area, there had to be a better means of traveling back and forth and moving supplies and agricultural products between the East and the West.

In European countries such as Holland, France, Germany, Italy, and England, canals had proved to be an effective and inexpensive means of transportation. The first canal in New York was begun in 1792. The original plan was to create an uninterrupted water route from the Hudson River to Lake Ontario by linking the Mohawk River, Oneida Lake, and the Oneida River. In the end, all that was built was a one-mile canal that enabled ships to get around Little Falls on the Mohawk River. However, in 1807, a man named Jesse Hawley came up with an idea for a canal that he thought would benefit many people.

Hawley was a flour merchant in Geneva, New York. He had to pay such high prices to transport his flour by wagon that he couldn't make any money. In 1807, after several months of studying maps of New York State, Hawley figured out a route for a canal connecting Lake Erie in western New York with the Hudson River in the eastern part of the state. This would provide a cheap, fast way to ship goods to settlers around the Great Lakes and in the Louisiana Purchase. Supplies such as crockery, sugar, molasses, coffee, nails, spikes, iron, and steel would travel up the Hudson River from New York City, across the state on the canal, then across the Great Lakes to settlers. Agricultural products from the settlers would follow the route in the opposite direction to reach the eastern markets. Hawley published essays about his idea in the *Genesee Messenger* in 1807 and 1808. A New York politician named De Witt Clinton read Hawley's essays in the newspaper and decided that Hawley was right.

TIMELINE

1808 — Jesse Hawley proposes canal to link Lake Erie and the Hudson River.

1817 — De Witt Clinton is elected governor of New York State. He persuades the legislature to authorize $7 million to build the Erie Canal proposed by Hawley. Construction begins. Benjamin Wright is hired as chief engineer, James Geddes as assistant chief engineer, and Nathan S. Roberts as assistant engineer.

1819 — Section of canal between Rome, New York, and Utica, New York, opens. Champlain Canal between Hudson and St. Lawrence Rivers opens.

1820 — Planning begins for "flight of five" at Lockport.

1825 — Erie Canal opens with celebrations all across the state.

1826–1831 — More canals open in New York, Pennsylvania, and New Jersey.

1835 — Enlargement of Erie Canal begins. Construction of Erie Railway begins.

TIMELINE

1836 — Utica and Schenectady Railroad completed. State of New York forbids it to carry freight to prevent it from competing with Erie Canal.

1862 — Enlargement of Erie Canal completed.

1882 — State of New York abolishes tolls on Erie Canal to help it compete with railroads.

1895 — Second enlargement of Erie Canal begins. It ends after three years because of lack of money.

1905 — Work begins on much larger Erie Barge Canal, which will replace old Erie Canal.

1918 — Erie Barge Canal completed.

1994 — Commercial traffic ceases on Erie Barge Canal.

1996 — New York State Canal Corporation approves spending $32 million to improve Erie Barge Canal for recreational use.

CHAPTER 1

THE BIG DITCH

In 1810, De Witt Clinton became the canal commissioner of New York. To raise public support for a canal throughout the state, Clinton gave speeches and wrote a letter to the state legislature. In spite of his efforts, many people thought the idea was foolish, calling it "Clinton's Folly" or "Clinton's Ditch." Nonetheless, Clinton remained convinced that it would work. When he was elected governor of New York in 1817, he persuaded the state legislature to authorize $7 million to build the canal. Work on the canal began later that year.

In the portrait on the next page, Clinton comes across as a great leader. He wears the plain, dark clothing favored by gentlemen of his time. The light tones of Clinton's face and hands stand out against the darker background. The artist did this intentionally to draw the viewer's attention to these features. Clinton's face wears a serious and thoughtful expression. The books on the table and the papers Clinton holds in his hand indicate that he is an educated man who believes in the value of study.

An unknown artist painted this portrait of Clinton sometime in the first quarter of the nineteenth century. As was common in portraits of prominent men, Clinton is shown standing. The viewer can see more than half of his body, but not all of it. This is called a three-quarter-length figure. The portrait shows the influence of what was called the New York portrait style, which was popular in the early 1800s. In this style, the colors used in the portrait always included red and black.

The Roman column partially visible behind Clinton reminds viewers that America's founding fathers looked to the Roman Republic as a model that our government and political leaders should copy. The red dye used for the curtain and the fabric of the chair behind Clinton suggests that he is a wealthy, powerful man. The best red dye at the time was made by grinding up insects that lived in the prickly pear cactus and was so rare that one pound of dye cost one pound of gold.

"Clinton's Ditch" was finished in 1825, and a great celebration to mark the canal's completion began on October 26 and continued for nine days. In Buffalo, Governor Clinton led a parade of nearly all of the city's 5,000 residents down to the western end of the "grand canal." After giving speeches, Governor Clinton, Lieutenant Governor James Tallmadge Jr., and other distinguished citizens of the state boarded a canal boat named the *Seneca Chief* and set off for New York City. On the journey, Clinton carried a keg of water from Lake Erie; he would pour it into the Atlantic Ocean in a ceremony when they reached New York Harbor. Cannons had been placed every ten miles along the canal. When the *Seneca Chief* began its journey, the first cannon was fired. When the men at the second cannon heard the noise of the first cannon, they fired their cannon. Eighty minutes later, the last cannon fired in New York City.

Towns across the state celebrated the Erie Canal. The broadside on the next page announces a "grand celebration" to be held in the town of Geneva. At the top is the date the Erie Canal was begun and the date for the official state ceremony marking its opening. The broadside describes the plans for Geneva's celebration, which included a public dinner and a public ball. Residents were asked to light up their houses in the evening. An artillery company would fire a salute, and bells would ring out as the salute

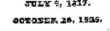

Broadsides are single sheets of paper, printed only on one side, that were meant to provide information to the public. They were posted around town or handed out to people in town squares, taverns, and churches. They were printed as quickly and cheaply as possible, and were meant to be thrown away after they had been read. As a result, broadsides are rare today. See page 54 for a transcription.

was fired. At the bottom of the broadside are the names of the men responsible for planning the events.

Because of the Erie Canal's importance, the broadside has been decorated with a fancy border and images at the top. Above the dates is an oval with a picture of George Washington, America's first president. Below the dates is an image of a canal boat being pulled by a horseback rider on the towpath.

On November 4, 1825, nine days after leaving Buffalo, the *Seneca Chief* reached New York Harbor. A magnificent ceremony marked the boat's arrival. More than 100,000 people crowded the shores. Clinton made a speech and then poured the keg of Lake Erie water into the Atlantic Ocean. This "marriage of the waters" symbolized the joining of Lake Erie and the Atlantic Ocean by the Erie Canal. Eighty years later, Charles Yardley Turner painted his interpretation of this historic event, which is shown on page 13.

Clinton is standing at the edge of a pier, holding the keg of water up high as he pours. Behind him to the right, an impressive crowd of well-dressed men is gathered. Some are in military uniform, and one man wears judge's robes. Everyone's attention is focused on Clinton as he pours the water from the keg.

A looped and knotted American flag is draped across the end of the pier, reminding the viewer that the Erie Canal is important to the entire nation and not just to New York. Behind Clinton, to the left, is a large steamboat, one of the nearly 150 ships that gathered in the harbor to greet the *Seneca Chief*. Barely visible beyond the steamboat is the skyline of New York City, soon to become the largest and wealthiest city in the nation as a result of the Erie Canal.

This painting, *Marriage of the Waters*, is one of two murals celebrating the Erie Canal that Charles Yardley Turner painted in 1905 for De Witt Clinton High School in New York City. The other mural, *Entering the Mohawk Valley*, shows a group of people standing and sitting on the prow of a canal boat. Turner was a well-known artist whose paintings included murals done for New York City courthouses and grand hotels. Murals are paintings on walls and are usually very large. Turner's Erie Canal murals, which are about twelve and a half feet tall and fifteen and three-quarters feet wide, were painted on canvas and then attached to the wall. When Turner painted these murals, the canal was being enlarged for a third time so that it would be able to handle the larger commercial ships that were then in use.

CHAPTER 2

The Erie Canal presented one of the greatest engineering challenges of its time. Before 1817, no one had ever built a canal longer than thirty miles. The Erie Canal was more than twelve times this long—it stretched 363 miles from Albany to Buffalo. The engineers involved in the project had to invent machines in order to solve the construction problems facing them.

AN ENGINEERING MARVEL

For example, they had to clear the land before construction could begin. To facilitate this, the engineers designed a machine that made it possible for one man working alone to bring down a tree quickly, without using a saw or an ax. This was achieved in the following way: One end of a cable was attached to the top of a tree, while the other end was attached to a special type of screw. The cable was wound around the screw by turning a wheel. Turning the wheel pulled the top of the tree lower and lower, until finally the tree came down.

The men who solved these problems had not been trained in the engineering skills needed to build canal structures. Some of them had other engineering experience. Others had worked as surveyors. All of them had to learn how to build canals as they went along. This led some people to nickname the canal project the "Erie School of Engineers." The "graduates" of this school went on to build the nation's network of canals and early railroads.

Benjamin Wright, the chief engineer on the Erie Canal, was born in Wethersfield, Connecticut, in 1770. He didn't have much formal education. However, he studied law with an uncle and eventually became a judge. There were no law schools in the country at that time, and most lawyers learned law through private study. Wright's uncle also taught him how to survey, or measure, land. Land had to be surveyed before it could be bought or sold. Wright was known as an accurate and honest surveyor, and it was because of his skills and reputation that he was chosen to be chief engineer.

The portrait of Wright on the next page testifies to his success. During this time, only wealthy, important people had their portraits painted. However, Wright's portrait features none of the lavish furnishings and objects representing success and wealth that are present in Clinton's portrait. Instead, the painting forces the viewer to focus on Wright himself. Because his face takes up most of the picture area, the viewer feels as though he or she is standing very close to him. The plain background doesn't draw the viewer's attention away from Wright's face. Wright seems to look straight at the viewer, with a hint of a smile on his lips, as though he's greeting an old friend.

After completing the Erie Canal, Wright went on to design and build many other canals, such as the Chesapeake and Ohio Canal and the Delaware and Hudson Canal. He was also one of the first men to design and build railroads, and he served as chief engineer of the Erie Railroad. Wright, who died in 1842, is known today as the "Father of American Civil Engineering."

James Geddes, the assistant chief engineer on the project, was born near Carlisle, Pennsylvania, in 1763. His father was a wealthy farmer, and the younger Geddes received the best education

This portrait of Benjamin Wright, painted by an unknown artist, is not dated. Wright looks to be somewhere between forty-five and sixty-five, which suggests that the portrait was probably painted between about 1815 and 1835. It is modest compared to many portraits of other notable people of the time. Such portraits commonly show at least a half-length figure; that is, they show the person from the waist up. Often they show a full-length figure, either standing or seated. These portraits usually include a grand setting, rich fabrics, and books or papers that tell us about the sitter's wealth, importance, and education. This portrait now belongs to one of Wright's descendants.

possible. After several years of traveling around the eastern United States, teaching, and running a salt-manufacturing business, Geddes went to work as a surveyor. Like Wright, he had a reputation for accuracy, and because of this he was chosen to be the assistant chief engineer for the Erie Canal.

Like Wright's portrait, the one of Geddes on page 18 is modest. However, Geddes doesn't look straight at the viewer the way Wright does. Instead, the artist has depicted him gazing into the distance, perhaps lost in his own thoughts. As a result, the viewer does not get the feeling of standing in front of the actual person, as occurs with the portrait of Wright.

Similar to Wright, Geddes later worked on other canals. He was chief engineer for the Ohio Canal and he also worked on the Pennsylvania canals. He died in 1838. A biography of Geddes was included in Joshua V. H. Clark's book, *Onondaga; or Reminiscences of Earlier and Later Times*, Vol. 2, published in Syracuse, New York, in 1849 by Stoddard and Babcock. Clark praised Geddes with these words: "His name will ever be associated with the noblest works of the age."

Nathan S. Roberts (pictured on page 20) was born in Piles Grove, New Jersey, in 1776. In 1817, he was made an assistant engineer on the Erie Canal. Soon thereafter, he was put in charge of the Rome to Rochester section of the canal. Drawn by the beauty of the area, Roberts purchased a farm located near the canal in Lenox, New York, about fifteen miles east of Syracuse. He remained there until his death in 1852.

In 1822, Roberts was given the task of finding a solution to one of the greatest obstacles faced by the Erie Canal engineers. Near Niagara Falls, in the western part of New York State, a sharply rising rock cliff soared more than seventy feet

In this portrait, James Geddes appears to be in his forties or fifties. This suggests that the artist, who is unknown, painted the portrait between about 1800 and 1820. Geddes is posed according to a set of rules for portraits that dates back to the Renaissance of the 1300s, 1400s, and 1500s. His body and head are turned slightly to one side in a three-quarters pose. In this type of pose, the viewer sees more of the face than would be the case in a profile pose, which would show one side, or one-half, of the sitter's face. However, the viewer sees less of Geddes's face than if his entire, or full, face was turned to look directly out from the painting.

above the surrounding land. To reach Lake Erie, the engineers had to find a way to get boats up and over this high ridge.

Normally, engineers use a lock to enable boats to move between sections of a canal with different water levels. A lock has a set of gates at each end. A boat going from a lower level to a higher level enters the lock through the lower gates, which are then closed behind it. Water is let into the lock to raise the boat to the level of the higher section. Then the gates at that end of the lock are opened, and the boat passes through. The process is reversed for boats moving from the higher level to the lower level. Double locks are like a two-way street, with one "lane" for boat traffic moving in one direction and another for boats moving in the opposite direction.

Roberts knew that it wouldn't be possible to reach the top of the seventy-foot cliff with a single pair of locks. Accordingly, he designed a series of five double locks that resembled a giant flight of stairs. Nothing this difficult had ever been done before, and Roberts's "flight of five" became one of the canal's great wonders. Remnants of the eastbound side survive, but they are not in use; the westbound side was replaced in 1918 with a flight of two locks that handle traffic in both directions.

Another problem the engineers faced was how to get across rivers and creeks, including the Genesee River, Irondequoit Creek, and Ninemile Creek. The solution was an aqueduct bridge. An aqueduct bridge had to be wide enough for the canal itself and for the towpath along the side of it. Canal boats didn't have engines or sails. Instead, they were towed by teams of horses or mules that walked beside the canal.

The Erie Canal required eighteen aqueduct bridges. One of the longest crossed the Genesee River at Rochester. Over 800 feet long, it was built of huge stones, all of which had to be quarried and shaped by hand. Like the "flight of five," the bridge at Rochester was admired as one of the most amazing accomplishments of the canal.

The canal created such excitement that there was a great demand for images of it. Artists made paintings, drawings, woodcuts, engravings, lithographs, and photographs of the canal. Sometimes, people wanted a picture as a souvenir of a trip on the canal or of a visit to one of the towns along the way. Other times, people wanted a picture because they wanted to see the

This portrait of Nathan S. Roberts by an unknown artist was probably done between about 1830 and 1840. As in the portrait of Wright, Roberts seems to be looking directly at the viewer. Unlike Wright, Roberts does not greet the viewer with a warm and welcoming gaze. His eyebrows are drawn together in a way that makes him look stern. Based on Roberts's demeanor, a viewer may well get the feeling that he or she has interrupted the engineer in the middle of important work and that Roberts does not want to be disturbed.

remarkable construction that everyone was talking about even though they could not visit it themselves. To meet this demand, pictures began to appear almost immediately after the canal opened.

Some of the Erie Canal's extraordinary features, such as the aqueduct bridge at Rochester, appeared repeatedly in images. In the woodcut shown on the next page, the aqueduct is in the center front, so it can be clearly seen. A team of horses pulls a boat across the aqueduct bridge as a second boat and team of horses approaches. The large, neat, and orderly houses of Rochester seen in the distance testify to the prosperity the canal brought to communities along its route. Within about fifteen years after the canal opened, Rochester had become a flourishing town of 20,000.

The first images of the canal were black-and-white prints, like the woodcut of the aqueduct at Rochester. These images often appeared in travel guides and magazines. Before long, artists were painting pictures based on sketches they had made while traveling on the canal. One of the first artists to record the canal in paintings was John William Hill. Between 1829 and 1831, Hill made several small watercolor paintings of scenes along the Erie Canal.

E. Peck, printer.

This woodcut of an aqueduct bridge was printed in the mid-1820s by Everard Peck, publisher of the *Rochester Telegraph*. It may have been made before the aqueduct was completed. Only seven of the eleven supporting arches are shown, and the iron railing that was put up along the outer edge of the towpath does not appear. To make a woodcut, the image is first drawn on a block of wood. Then all the areas between and around the lines are cut away, so that what remains are the raised lines of the design. Ink is rubbed or rolled on the raised area, then the block is pressed against paper to create the final print. Hundreds of copies of an image can be printed with this technique.

In the watercolor on page 23, which is only slightly larger than a piece of notebook paper, Hill provides much information about life along the canal. Near the bottom right of the painting, a bearded man drives a sow, or female pig, and her piglets down a road that crosses the canal. On the canal is a packet boat with a few passengers visible on top. These small boats could be run by a crew of only four men, who were known as "canawlers": the captain, steersman, cook, and "hoggee," who handled the mules that towed the boat. The hoggee is on the left, riding a white horse and driving the horses along the towpath. Behind the hoggee, sheep graze in a fenced meadow. Beyond that is a cluster of well-kept houses. The peaceful scene and warm, golden light suggest that life along the canal was good.

Like the aqueduct bridge at Rochester, the "flight of five" near Niagara Falls frequently appeared in engravings, paintings, photos, and drawings. The engraving on page 24 illustrates how much this community had grown since December 1820, when there were only three log cabins in the area. A mere three years later, the locks had attracted many people and businesses. The engraving presents the view seen from the top of the highest lock, looking east down the canal. Along the front of the picture, near the center, is the upper lock for boats headed east, toward Albany. The two large wooden arms that form a V shape across the lock are the levers for opening and closing the gate. Two men stand at one arm, ready to open it when needed. Just above the right arm, the arms for the lower four locks are barely visible. Above the V of the lock arms, a man stands on a footbridge across the lock, watching boat traffic on the canal below. In the lower left corner of the engraving, a boat is in the upper

John William Hill (1812–1879) was only about seventeen when he painted this scene in 1829. It is one of several small watercolors he did of the canal between 1829 and 1831. His father, John Hill, was an engraver, and John William helped in his father's studio from 1822 until 1829. John William Hill started his career as a landscape painter, carefully recording the precise features of each place he painted. This watercolor is an example of his early landscape paintings. Because of the care with which he painted landscapes, he was hired in 1836 to work for the state of New York, making realistic paintings of different parts of the state. He did this work until 1841.

lock for traffic heading west, toward Buffalo. A man atop the boat holds a long pole for pushing the boat away from the lock walls if necessary.

When construction of the locks began in 1823, some 1,200 laborers, mostly Irish immigrants who were already in New York, came to work on the project. To provide the goods and services the workers needed, merchants, farmers, doctors, and bankers soon arrived. By the time the Erie Canal opened in 1825, a town of 2,500 people had grown up around the locks. The town took its name from its famous locks and was called Lockport.

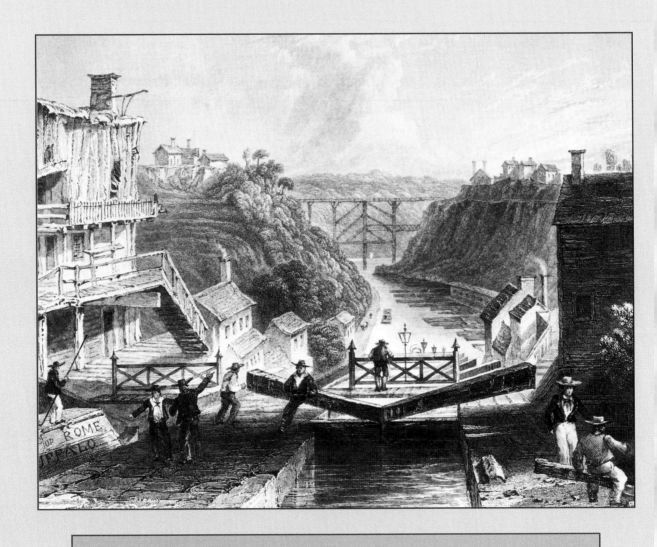

This engraving, from 1839, is based on a drawing made by William H. Bartlett (1809–1854), an English landscape artist who was famous for his images of places all over the world. Bartlett gave his drawing to an engraver, who copied each image onto a steel plate using special tools. The tools cut deep lines into the plate, and then the printer rubs ink into the lines. When the inked plate, covered with a piece of printing paper, is rolled through a printing press, the image from the plate transfers onto the piece of paper. An image on an engraved plate can be run through a press hundreds of times before the quality of the image deteriorates.

Bartlett made several trips to the United States to make drawings for the engravings that were included in a book of landscapes called *American Scenery*, written by N. P. Willis. The book, featuring the above engraving, was published in London by George Virtue in 1840.

During the second and third quarters of the nineteenth century, the Erie Canal was such a popular subject that canal scenes could be found decorating plates, cups, bowls, wallpaper, and clothing. One man who worked on the canal even had a picture of an aqueduct carved on his gravestone.

CHAPTER 3

THE CANAL AGE

The section of the Erie Canal between Rome and Utica opened in October 1819. Its immediate success helped fuel a canal-building fever. The Champlain Canal, connecting the Hudson and St. Lawrence Rivers, also opened in 1819; in 1826, a canal connecting Cayuga and Seneca Lakes with the Erie Canal was completed; two years later came the Oswego Canal, linking Lake Ontario and the Erie Canal system; in 1828, the Delaware and Hudson Canal opened, joining the coalfields of Pennsylvania to the Hudson River; and in 1831, the Morris Canal in New Jersey opened, joining the Delaware River to the Hudson River. The communities along these canals grew and prospered.

The Morris Canal in New Jersey was built by the Morris Canal and Banking Company. The State of New Jersey gave the company permission to print its own canal money, shown on page 27, which would be used to pay the tolls on the canal. Lavish decoration on the money includes Roman gods and goddesses associated with water, abundance, and celebration. These figures were chosen because nineteenth-century Americans admired ancient Rome and its engineering accomplishments, such as aqueducts, roads, and public baths.

At the top of the bill, in the center, is Minerva, the Roman goddess of wisdom. According to one story, Minerva visited a sacred spring that flowed from a rock after it had been struck by the hoof

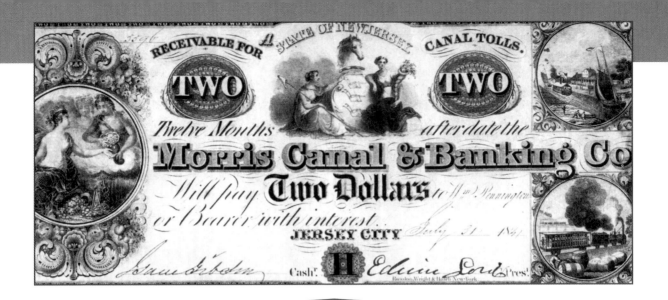

Like the money in use today, this canal money—issued in 1841—is actually an engraving, produced the same way as Bartlett's engraving of Lockport on page 24. Examining a modern dollar bill with a magnifying glass will indicate exactly how much work and skill are required to make money; hundreds of lines—some thin, some thick, some thick in the middle and thin at the ends—need to be painstakingly engraved into a metal plate. In a lot of bills, including the canal money, the network of lines is so complicated that it is very difficult to copy. This is done on purpose to prevent forgery.

of the winged horse, Pegasus. The head of Pegasus appears above Minerva's shield. The woman to the right of the shield holds a cornucopia, or horn of plenty. Historians can't decide whether this woman is Ceres, the goddess of abundance, or Fortune, who was associated with occasions worthy of public celebration. A river god and goddess appear in the large circle on the left side of the money.

Along the right side are images of the flourishing trade made possible by the Morris Canal. A canal scene is in the top circle. Beneath it is a train; trains were often required for at least part of the journey to transport goods (and people) from place to place.

The Erie Canal was a huge success even before it was completed. In 1824, traffic on the sections that were open allowed New York State to collect $300,000 in tolls. In 1826, the first full year the entire canal was open for business, the state collected more than

$1 million in tolls—an exceptional amount of money, especially in the 1800s. More than 185,000 tons of agricultural products, such as wheat, flour, bacon, butter, cheese, corn, and potatoes, were transported from Buffalo to Albany in 1826, and more than 32,000 tons of manufactured goods, such as furniture, nails, iron, steel, and crockery, traveled from Albany to Buffalo. By 1845, more than one million tons of freight went up and down the canal annually.

To find out how much to charge for different kinds of freight, toll collectors used rate charts like the one on page 29. The rates were based on three factors: distance, weight of the freight, and type of freight. The highest tolls were charged for luxury items, such as silverware, china, and fabrics like silk and velvet. The lowest tolls were for items such as brick, sand, clay, and manure.

The chart is divided into two sides, each with information arranged in clearly labeled columns. The left side of the chart lists rates for agricultural products shipped from Buffalo to Albany. It also lists the distance from Buffalo to each port along the canal. The right side indicates rates for manufactured goods shipped from Albany to Buffalo and the distance from Albany to each port. Rates are calculated in monetary units called mills; a mill is equal to one-tenth of a cent.

Sometimes distance and rate information were divided into separate tables, as in the example on page 30. The distance table, titled "A List of the Principal Places on the Erie Canal, and Their Distance from Each Other," is arranged with Albany as the starting point, at the top of the "Names of Places" column, and Buffalo as the final stop, listed on the right at the bottom of the column. To figure out what the toll would be for a particular type of freight, you first had to look at the table of distances to find out how many miles the freight would be traveling. Then you would look at the toll rates to

TABLE OF THE NEW RATES OF TOLL

ON THE ERIE CANAL,

As established by the Canal board, and in effect on said Canal.

Produce, &c.

Miles.		Toll of a bbl Flour. (C M F)	100 lbs 4. m. (C M F)	100 lbs 3. m. (C M F)	100 lbs 2. m. (C M F)	100 lbs 1. m. (C M F)
0	BUFFALO.					
3	Black Rock,	025.9.0	012	009	006	003
4	Lower Black Rock,	034.5.6	016	012	008	004
12	Tonawanda,	103.6.8	048	036	024	012
18	H. Brockway's,	155.5.2	072	054	036	018
23	Welch's,	198.7.2	092	069	046	023
24	Pendleton,	207.3.6	096	076	048	024
31	Lockport,	267.8.4	124	093	062	031
37	Orange Port,	319.6.8	148	111	074	037
38	Gasport,	328.3.2	152	114	076	038
40	Reynold's Basin,	345.6.0	160	120	080	040
43	Middleport,	371.5.2	172	129	086	043
46	Shelby Basin,	397.4.4	184	138	092	046
49	Medina,	423.3.6	196	147	098	049
52	Road Culvert,	449.2.8	208	156	104	052
53	Knowlesville,	457.9.2	212	159	106	053
55	Long Bridge,	475.2.0	220	165	110	055
57	Eagle Harbor,	492.4.8	228	171	114	057
58	Gaines' Basin,	501.1.2	232	174	116	058
60	Albion,	518.4.0	240	180	120	060
64	Hindsburgh,	552.9.6	256	192	128	064
66	Hulberton,	570.2.4	264	198	132	066
70	Holley,	604.8.0	280	210	140	070
75	Brockport,	648.0.0	300	225	150	075
77	Cooley's Basin,	665.2.8	308	231	154	077
80	Adams' Basin,	691.2.0	320	240	160	080
83	Spencer's Basin,	717.1.2	332	249	166	083
85	Brockway's	734.4.0	340	255	170	085
95	Rochester,	820.8.0	380	285	190	095
99	Lock No. 3,	855.3.6	396	297	198	099
101	Billinghast's Basin,	872.6.4	404	303	202	101
105	Pittsford,	907.2.0	420	315	210	105
108	Bushnell's Basin,	933.1.2	432	324	216	108
111	Fullam's Basin,	959.0.4	444	333	222	111
112	Fairport,	967.6.8	448	336	224	112
113	Perrinton centre,	976.3.2	452	339	226	113
115	Perrinton,	993.6.0	460	345	230	115
117	Wayneport,	1010.8.8	468	351	234	117
120	Macedonville,	1036.8.0	480	360	240	120
124	Palmyra,	1071.3.6	496	372	248	124
129	Port Gibson,	1114.5.6	516	387	258	129
132	Newark,	1140.4.8	528	396	264	132
133	Lockville,	1149.1.2	532	399	266	133
139	Lyons,	1200.9.6	556	417	278	139
143	Lock Berlin,	1235.5.2	572	429	286	143
148	Clyde,	1278.7.2	592	444	296	148
153	Lockpit,	1321.9.2	612	459	306	153
159	Montezuma,	1373.7.6	636	477	318	159
165	Port Byron,	1425.6.0	660	495	330	165
167	Centreport,	1442.8.8	668	501	334	167
168	Weedsport,	1451.5.2	672	504	336	168
173	Cold Spring,	1494.7.2	692	519	346	173
174	Jordan,	1503.3.6	696	522	348	174
178	Peru,	1537.9.2	712	534	356	178
180	Canton,	1555.2.0	720	540	360	180
185	Camillus,	1598.4.0	740	555	370	185
186	Nine Mile Creek,	1607.0.4	744	558	372	186
187	Bellisle,	1615.6.8	748	561	374	187
191	Geddes,	1650.2.4	764	573	382	191
193	Syracuse,	1667.5.2	772	579	386	193
194	Lodi,	1676.1.6	776	582	388	194
199	Orville Feeder,	1719.3.6	796	597	398	199
201	Limestone Feeder, (Hall's Landing.)	1736.6.4	804	603	402	201
202	Manlius,	1745.2.8	808	606	404	202
204	Little Lake,	1762.5.6	816	612	408	204
206	Kirkville,	1779.8.4	824	618	412	206
208	Pool's Brook,	1797.1.2	832	624	416	208
211	Chittenango,	1823.0.4	844	633	422	211
214	New Boston,	1848.9.6	856	642	428	214
218	Canastota,	1883.5.2	872	654	436	218
222	Oneida Creek, [Durhamville.]	1918.0.8	888	666	444	222
226	Loomis',	1952.6.4	904	678	452	226
228	Higgins',	1969.9.2	912	684	456	228
232	New London,	2004.4.8	928	696	464	232
234	Stony Creek,	2021.7.6	936	702	468	234
235	Hawley's Basin,	2030.4.0	940	705	470	235
237	Wood Cr'k Aqueduct [Fort Bull.]	2047.6.8	948	711	474	237
239	Rome,	2064.9.6	956	717	478	239
247	Oriskany,	2134.0.8	988	741	494	247
250	Whitesboro',	2160.0.0	1000	750	500	250
251	York Mills,	2168.6.4	1004	753	502	251
254	Utica,	2194.5.6	1016	762	508	254
257	Ferguson's,	2220.4.8	1028	771	514	257
263	Frankfort,	2272.3.2	1052	789	526	263
265	Steel's Creek,	2289.6.0	1060	795	530	265
266	Morgan's Landing,	2298.2.4	1064	798	532	266
267	Fulmer's Creek,	2306.8.8	1068	801	534	267
268	Mohawk,	2315.5.2	1072	804	536	268
269	Herkimer lo'r br'ge,	2324.1.6	1076	807	538	269
273	Rankins, L'k No. 7,	2358.7.2	1092	819	546	273
276	Little Falls,	2384.6.4	1104	828	552	276
278	Fink's Ferry,	2401.9.2	1112	834	556	278
281	Indian Castle, [Nowandaga Creek.]	2427.8.4	1124	843	562	281
283	East Canada Creek,	2445.1.2	1132	849	566	283
287	St. Johnsville,	2479.6.8	1148	861	574	287
289	Diefendorf's Land'g	2496.9.6	1156	867	578	289
292	Fort Plain,	2522.8.8	1168	876	584	292
295	Canajoharie,	2548.8.0	1180	885	590	295
298	Spraker's Basin,	2574.7.2	1192	894	596	298
300	Big Nose,	2592.0.0	1200	900	600	300
307	Fultonville,	2652.4.8	1228	921	614	307
310	Smithtown,	2678.4.0	1240	930	620	310
312	Schoharie Creek,	2695.6.8	1248	936	624	312
317	Amsterdam, [Port Jackson.]	2738.8.8	1268	951	634	317
319	Florida,	2756.1.6	1276	957	638	319
320	Phillip's Locks,	2764.8.0	1280	960	640	320
325	Rotterdam,	2808.0.0	1300	975	650	325
334	Schenectady,	2885.7.6	1336	1002	668	334
338	Upper Aqueduct,	2920.3.2	1352	1014	676	338
345	Willow Spring,	2980.8.0	1380	1035	690	345
351	Lower Aqueduct,	3032.6.4	1404	1053	702	351
354	Cohoes,	3058.5.6	1416	1062	708	354
357	West Troy,	3084.4.8	1428	1071	714	357
358	Gibbonsville,	3093.1.2	1432	1074	716	358
359	Port Schuyler,	3101.7.6	1436	1077	718	359
364	ALBANY.	3144.9.6	1456	1092	728	364

Merchandize Furn't.

Miles.		100 lbs 8. m. (C M F)	100 lbs 5. m. (C M F)	100 lbs 3. m. (C M F)
0	ALBANY.			
5	Port Schuyler,	040	025	015
6	Gibbonsville,	048	030	018
7	West Troy,	056	035	021
10	Cohoes,	080	050	030
13	Lower Aqueduct,	104	065	039
19	Willow Spring,	152	095	057
26	Upper Aqueduct,	208	130	078
30	Schenectady,	240	150	090
39	Rotterdam,	312	195	117
44	Phillip's Locks,	352	220	132
45	Florida,	360	225	135
47	Amsterdam, [Port Jackson.]	376	235	141
52	Schoharie Creek,	416	260	156
54	Smithtown,	432	270	162
57	Fultonville,	456	285	171
64	Big Nose,	512	320	192
66	Spraker's Basin,	528	330	198
69	Canajoharie,	552	345	207
72	Fort Plain,	576	360	216
75	Diefendorf's Land'g	600	375	225
77	St. Johnsville,	616	385	231
81	East Canada Creek,	648	405	243
83	Indian Castle, [Nowandaga Creek.]	664	415	249
86	Fink's Ferry,	688	430	258
88	Little Falls,	704	440	264
91	Rankin's L'k No. 7,	728	455	273
95	Herkimer lo'r br'ge,	760	475	285
96	Mohawk,	768	480	288
97	Fulmer's Creek,	776	485	291
98	Morgan's Landing,	784	490	294
99	Steele's Creek,	792	495	297
101	Frankfort,	808	505	303
107	Ferguson's,	856	535	321
110	Utica,	880	550	330
113	York Mills,	904	565	339
114	Whitesboro',	912	570	342
117	Oriskany,	936	585	351
125	Rome,	1000	625	375
127	Wood C'k Aqueduct [Fort Bull.]	1016	635	381
129	Hawley's Basin,	1032	645	387
130	Stony Creek,	1040	650	390
132	New London,	1056	660	396
136	Higgins',	1088	680	408
138	Loomis',	1104	690	414
141	Oneida Creek, [Durhamville.]	1128	705	423
146	Canastota,	1168	730	438
150	New Boston,	1200	750	450
153	Chittenango,	1224	765	459
156	Pool's Brook,	1248	780	468
158	Kirkville,	1264	790	474
160	Little Lake,	1280	800	480
162	Manlius,	1296	810	486
163	Limestone Feeder, [Hall's Landing.]	1304	815	489
165	Orville Feeder,	1320	825	495
170	Lodi,	1360	850	510
171	Syracuse,	1368	855	513
173	Geddes,	1384	865	519
177	Bellisle,	1416	885	531
178	Nine Mile Creek,	1424	890	534
179	Camillus,	1432	895	537
184	Canton,	1472	920	552
186	Peru,	1488	930	558
190	Jordan,	1520	950	570
191	Cold Spring,	1528	955	573
196	Weedsport,	1568	980	588
197	Centreport,	1576	985	591
199	Port Byron,	1592	995	597
205	Montezuma,	1640	1025	615
211	Lockpit,	1688	1055	633
216	Clyde,	1728	1080	648
221	Lock Berlin,	1768	1105	663
225	Lyons,	1800	1125	675
231	Lockville,	1848	1155	693
232	Newark,	1856	1160	696
235	Port Gibson,	1880	1175	705
240	Palmyra,	1920	1200	720
244	Macedonville,	1952	1220	732
247	Wayneport,	1976	1235	741
249	Perrinton,	1992	1245	747
251	Perrinton Centre,	2008	1255	753
252	Fairport,	2016	1260	756
253	Fullam's Basin,	2024	1265	759
256	Bushnell's Basin,	2048	1280	768
259	Pittsford,	2072	1295	777
263	Billinghast's Basin,	2104	1315	789
265	Lock No. 3,	2120	1325	795
269	Rochester,	2152	1345	807
279	Brockway's,	2232	1395	837
281	Spencer's Basin,	2248	1405	843
284	Adams' Basin,	2272	1420	852
287	Cooley's Basin,	2296	1435	861
289	Brockport,	2312	1445	867
294	Holley,	2352	1470	882
298	Hulberton,	2384	1490	894
300	Hindsburgh,	2400	1500	900
304	Albion,	2432	1520	912
306	Gaines' Basin,	2448	1530	918
307	Eagle Harbor,	2456	1535	921
309	Long Bridge,	2472	1545	927
311	Knowlesville,	2488	1555	933
312	Road Culvert,	2496	1560	936
315	Medina,	2520	1575	945
318	Shelby Basin,	2544	1590	954
321	Middleport,	2568	1605	963
324	Reynolds' Basin,	2592	1620	972
326	Gasport,	2608	1630	978
327	Orange Port,	2616	1635	981
333	Lockport,	2664	1665	999
340	Pendleton,	2720	1700	1020
342	Welch's,	2736	1710	1026
346	H. Brockway's,	2768	1730	1038
352	Tonawanda,	2816	1760	1056
360	Lower Black Rock,	2880	1800	1080
361	Black Rock,	2888	1805	1083
364	BUFFALO.	2912	1820	1092

4 Mills. On flour, salted beef and pork, bacon, butter, cheese, tallow, lard, beer and cider, pot and pearl ashes, window glass or glass ware, manufactured in this State, kelp, charcoal, broken castings, scrap iron and pig iron, stove, and all other iron castings, except machines and parts thereof, copperas and manganese, going towards tide water, sheep skins, and raw hides of domestic animals of the United States, slate and tile for roofing, and stone ware, wool, rags and junk, manilla, wheat and all other agricultural productions of the United States not particularly specified, and not being merchandize, and all articles not enumerated or excepted, passing *towards* tide water.

3 Mills. On foreign gypsum, household furniture, carts, wagons, sleighs, ploughs and mechanics' tools, horses, (and each horse when not weighed to be computed at 900 lbs.) and corn.

2 Mills. On bran and ship stuffs, in bulk, stone, blocks of timber for paving streets, sawed lath, of less than ten feet in length, split lath, hoop poles, hand spikes, rowing oars, broom handles, spokes, hubs, tree-nails, felloes, boat knees, plane stocks, pickets for fences, and stuff manufactured or partly manufactured for chairs or bedsteads, and hop poles, brush handles, brush backs, looking glass backs, gun stocks, plough beams and plough handles, cotton, live cattle, sheep, hogs, horns, hoofs and bones, and pressed hay and pressed broom corn.

1 Mill. On gypsum, the product of this State, (not entitled to bounty,) brick, sand, lime, clay, earth, manure and iron ore, staves and heading, transported in boats, hemp and unmanufactured tobacco going towards tide water, and potatoes.

8 Mills. Merchandize not enumerated, and all other articles not enumerated or excepted, passing *from* tide water.

5 Mills. Sugar, molasses, coffee, nails, spikes, iron, steel, crockery.

3 Mills. On household furniture, accompanied by and actually belonging to families emigrating, carts, wagons, sleighs, ploughs and mechanics' tools necessary for the owner's individual use, when accompanied by the owner, emigrating for the purpose of settlement.

This table, printed in 1846, does not indicate the name of the printer. The table is a broadside. The toll collector would post the table in a spot in his office where it would be easiest for him to consult it and quickly find the information he needed. To enable the toll collector to find information quickly and easily, the charts were given a simple design. That's why the only decorative element on this chart is the fancy border. Because the tables were in constant use, they were easily damaged and frequently had to be replaced. New tables were printed when rates changed and the outdated tables were thrown away. Because of this, very few toll tables exist today. For more information on how to use the toll table, as well as a complete transcription of the key, see page 55 in the Primary Source Transcriptions section.

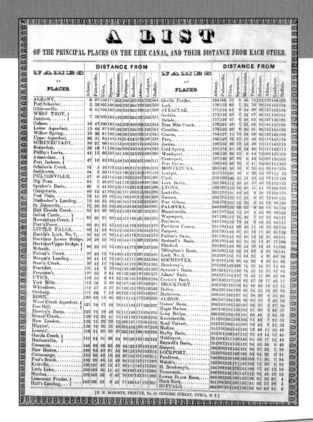

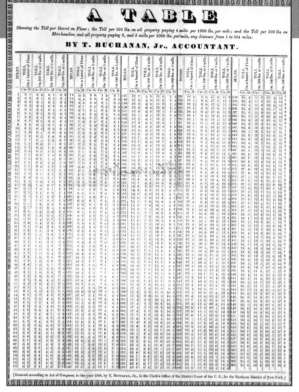

This leaflet contains a toll table and a table of the major towns and cities along the canal. It was printed in 1846 by R. W. Roberts (this is indicated at the bottom of the list of places), at No. 58 Genesee Street in Utica, New York. Leaflets such as these were probably handed out to canawlers and merchants instead of being used by toll collectors. The writing at the top of the toll table indicates that the information was gathered and written out for the printer by T. Buchanan Jr., accountant. Additional information about Buchanan appears at the bottom of the table. For more information on how these tables were used, see page 55 at the back of this book.

find out what the toll would be for that type of freight traveling that many miles.

With all the income that was collected from canal tolls, New York State became very wealthy. By 1836, New York had collected more than enough to cover the cost of building the canal. By 1846, the year these toll-rate tables were printed, the volume of traffic on the canal had reached staggering levels. The number of boats using the canal had grown from about 170 in 1826 to about 4,000 in 1846. The number of men employed on the boats and on the canal itself had reached about 25,000. Towns along the canal flourished. The population of Utica increased from about 3,000 to about 13,000 in only twenty years. Syracuse, which consisted of only a few wooden houses in 1820, had 11,000 residents in 1840. Buffalo, a tiny wilderness settlement of about 200 in 1812, had a population of 18,000 by 1840.

Recognizing the canal's importance to the state's economy, the New York legislature decided to enlarge the canal so that it could handle bigger boats carrying more freight. Work on this project started in 1835 but came to a halt during the Depression of 1837. Banks had been lending money to anyone who wanted it. When many people could not pay back the loans, the banks lost money. Then governments ran out of money to pay for projects like canals.

Some people in the state government thought that the state should abandon the enlargement of the canal because it was too expensive. Others thought the expansion was so important to the state that they should borrow money to pay for it. In 1853, map-maker David Vaughan, who made many official maps for the state, made the map of the eastern United States shown on page 32 to illustrate how the enlarged canal would benefit New York. The legend in the lower right-hand corner tells us that the map shows all the routes used to carry agricultural products from the northwest (today we call this region the Midwest) to the Atlantic coast. In addition, according to the legend, the map shows the positive effects that the state engineer believed the canal enlargement would have. For example, the bigger ships that the enlarged canal could handle would enable it to compete with the railroads in the region. The expanded canal would receive freight from a vast area, outlined in color on the map, and this would greatly increase the

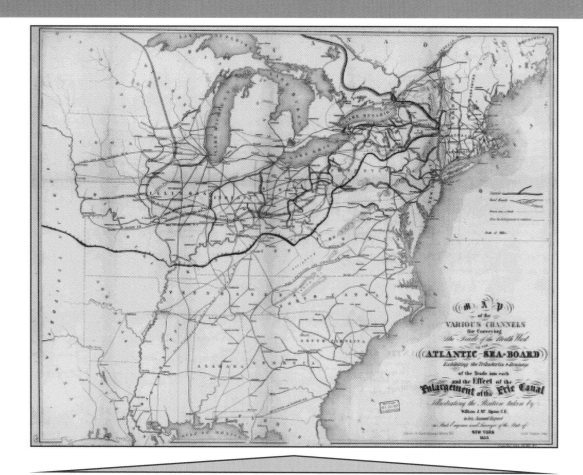

This 1853 map, entitled "Map of the Various Channels for Conveying the Trade of the North West to the Atlantic Sea-Board; Exhibiting the Tributaries & Drainage of the Trade into each, and the Effect of the Enlargement of the Erie Canal," was made in Albany, New York, by David Vaughan. Vaughan was a mapmaker, or cartographer, who made many official maps for the state of New York. This map accompanied the annual report of William J. McAlpine, New York State engineer and surveyor on the canals. The report was submitted to the state legislature on February 9, 1854.

toll revenues the state received. Finally, the legend notes that this map was part of the annual report that the state engineer submitted to the State of New York.

The map also shows canals, finished railroads, railroads under construction, and proposed railroads. Depicting canals and railroads together indicates how the two could be joined together to form long routes that would bring extra business to both. It also lets officials see that the expanding railroads threaten to take more and more business away from the Erie Canal, steadily decreasing the state's income from tolls. The way to make sure that the Erie Canal continued to compete successfully with the railroads was to enlarge the canal.

Work on the enlargement resumed in 1853. By 1860, commerce on the canal had increased greatly, as the weekly statement on page 34 shows. In the lower half of the statement, the collector recorded the quantities of different agricultural products delivered to West Troy on the canal. He reported the delivery of 33,004 barrels of flour in a single week, almost eight times the average number of barrels transported weekly in 1825. He also reported that an astonishing 1,040,860 bushels of wheat were delivered. This is almost double the amount transported in all of 1825. Altogether, almost two million tons of agricultural products were carried east from Buffalo in 1860. In 1825, only 185,000 tons of freight traveled east on the canal.

The increasing volume of freight yielded a huge financial benefit for New York State. In 1862, the year the enlargement of the Erie Canal was completed, the state collected more than $4,500,000 in tolls. Government officials and wealthy citizens in other states wanted to build canals that would help their states collect large sums of money, too.

In 1862, Isaac N. Arnold, a member of Congress from Illinois, wrote to President Abraham Lincoln about a proposal for a steamboat canal to connect Lake Michigan and the Mississippi River. Steamboats had hauled freight and passengers on the Great Lakes since 1816. A canal that linked Lake Michigan and the Mississippi River, thereby creating a continuous water route

[This return is to be made by the Collectors at New-York, Albany, West Troy and Waterford, and is to correspond with and accompany each weekly abstract.]

WEEKLY STATEMENT

Showing the quantity of the several articles First Cleared on the Canals at, and the quantity Left at West Troy for W S during the 4th week in Oct 1860

MERCHANDISE CLEARED.

ARTICLES.	On Erie Canal.	On Champlain Canal.	TOTAL.
Sugar at 2 mills,..........................pounds,			
Molasses, " .... "			
Coffee, " .... "			
Nails, " .... "			
Iron, " .... "			
Railroad Iron, " .... "			
All other merchandise at 2 mills,.......... "			
TOTAL,...........................			

	Left from Erie Canal.	Left from Champlain Canal.	TOTAL.
Flour,..........................barrels,	33,004		33,004
Wheat,..........................bushels,	1,040,860		1,040,860
Corn,.......................... "	131,583		131,583
Barley,.......................... "	150,607		150,607
Rye,.......................... "	18,113		18,113
Oats,.......................... "	639,976	3,000	642,976
Bran and Ship Stuffs,..........pounds,	1,200,600		1,200,600
Ashes,..........................barrels,	32		32
Beef,.......................... "	88		88
Pork,.......................... "			
Bacon,..........................pounds,			
Butter,.......................... "	1,087,400	300	1,087,700
Lard,.......................... "	40,100		40,100
Cheese,.......................... "	1,659,000	1,500	1,659,000
Wool,.......................... "	15,900		15,900
Domestic Spirits,..........gallons,	30,585		30,585

I CERTIFY the above to be correct,

W D Sunderlin
Collector.

Weekly statements were part of the reports the collectors at New York City, Albany, West Troy, and Waterford were required to submit to the Canal Board every week. According to the information at the top, this statement was for West Troy and covered the fourth week of October in 1860. W. D. Sunderlin, whose signature appears at the bottom, was the collector. The upper portion of the form, which deals with manufactured goods, is blank. The lower portion, which deals with agricultural products, shows huge quantities being delivered. Almost all the products reached West Troy on the Erie Canal. Only 3,000 bushels of oats, 300 pounds of butter, and 1,500 pounds of cheese were delivered on the Champlain Canal. It appears Sunderlin forgot to include the cheese delivered on the Champlain Canal when he calculated the totals, since the total figure given for cheese exactly equals the amount delivered on the Erie Canal alone.

Sunderlin recorded the following quantities of agricultural products arriving in West Troy from Buffalo by way of the Erie Canal: flour, 33,004 barrels; wheat, 1,040,860 bushels; corn, 131,583 bushels; barley, 150,507 bushels; rye, 18,113 bushels; oats, 639,976 bushels; bran and ship stuffs, 1,200,600 pounds; ashes, 32 barrels; beef, 88 barrels; butter, 1,087,400 pounds; lard, 40,100 pounds; cheese, 1,659,000 pounds; wool, 15,900 pounds; and domestic spirits, 30,585 gallons. Arriving on the Champlain Canal were 3,000 bushels of oats, 300 pounds of butter, and 1,500 pounds of cheese.

From 1861 until 1865, Isaac N. Arnold represented Illinois in Congress. Even after leaving Congress, he continued to be a prominent state figure. Arnold was a great admirer and close friend of Abraham Lincoln, and the two men wrote to each other often. In this letter, it's apparent that the way in which words are spelled has changed over time. For example, in the letter, "Nicessity" is used instead of the modern-day spelling "necessity," and "defences" is used instead of "defenses." Of equal interest, and also indicative of how the use of language has changed over time, is the fact that Arnold signed the letter "Respectfully," even though he and Lincoln were good friends. Regardless of their friendship, that was the proper and accepted way to sign a letter to the president. This letter is one of many written by Arnold that are now part of the Abraham Lincoln Papers at the Library of Congress in Washington, D.C. See page 56 for a transcription and a contemporary English translation.

from the Great Lakes to the Gulf of Mexico, would establish an enormous unified trade area.

Arnold suggested that if Lincoln addressed Congress about enlarging the Erie Canal, he could use that opportunity to talk about the steamboat canal as well. Arnold also noted that several committees in Congress had already given their support to the proposed steamboat canal and that the project would be easy to execute. Arnold hoped that the steamboat canal would bring the same benefits to Illinois and its largest city, Chicago, that the Erie Canal had brought to New York.

CHAPTER 4

The Erie Canal continued to prosper for several more years after the enlargement was completed. By 1868, the volume of freight carried by the canal exceeded three million tons. Increasingly, however, railroads were challenging the canals' control over the transportation of goods.

In the early years of the canal age, canals and trains often formed partnerships, creating routes covered partly by train and partly by canal boat. Though these partnerships also pertained to goods, they were espe-

COMPETITION FROM THE RAILROAD

cially beneficial to travelers. Packet boats allowed passengers to experience the wonders of the canals and enjoy the scenery. Trains, on the other hand, were faster—packet boats moved at a speed of only four miles per hour—and were often more comfortable. However, there were very few railroads, and those that existed covered only short distances.

New York's first railroad opened in 1831, stretching sixteen miles from Albany to Schenectady. An 1834 broadside (shown on page 37) advertises an arrangement between the railroad and packet boats on the Erie Canal. Passengers could take a train departing Albany at 9:00 AM or one departing at 5:00 PM. The morning train would get them to Schenectady in time to

This broadside, which now belongs to the Canal Society of New York State, would originally have been posted in public places such as town squares and taverns to advertise this travel arrangement. As an advertisement, it had to grab people's attention and be easy to read quickly. Interesting visuals were used to attract the attention of prospective customers. In addition, the printer used large typefaces so that it would be easy to read from a distance. Horizontal lines above and below the area with the pictures help to organize the broadside into sections, which also makes reading easier.

At the top of the broadside is a standard packet boat being pulled along the canal by a team of horses on the towpath. Below is the train that would carry travelers to the packet boat. At the right end of the train is the locomotive. The train engineer stands on an open platform at the rear of the locomotive. Behind the locomotive is the freight and baggage car, loaded high with suitcases, trunks, and a bundle labeled "wool." Next is a passenger car, with many passengers visible through the large open windows. At the end is a flatcar, with a carriage full of travelers resting on it.

catch the packet boat leaving for Utica, Rochester, and Buffalo at 10:30 AM. The afternoon train would allow passengers to catch the packet boat leaving Schenectady at 6:30 PM. By taking the train instead of the canal from Albany to Schenectady, travelers shortened their journey by one day.

In 1836, two years after the broadside was printed, the Utica and Schenectady Railroad was completed, making it possible to travel (or transport goods) all the way from Albany to Utica by train. The railroad ran right alongside the Erie Canal between the cities of Utica and Schenectady, and for the first time, the railroads were really competing with the canals. Alarmed by the prospect of trains taking business away from the canals, the New York State legislature passed a law that made it illegal for trains to carry freight. This ensured that all freight would be transported on the canals. As railroads became more common, however, attitudes changed. By the 1850s, the legislature allowed the Utica and Schenectady Railroad to carry freight.

In 1868—the year that the amount of freight transported on the Erie Canal exceeded three million tons—a map was created that illustrated all the canals and railroads in New York. The map (shown on page 39) traces the Erie Canal, arching north from Buffalo through Niagara County, and then snaking its way eastward across the state until it joins the Hudson River just north of Albany. Shorter canals that link other parts of the state to the Erie Canal also appear. Together, they create a canal system that connects all parts of the state.

The map also reveals the even larger network of railroads, which were quickly becoming a threat to the canal system. Railroads crisscrossed New York State and followed the northern coast of Lake Ontario in Canada; they reached down into

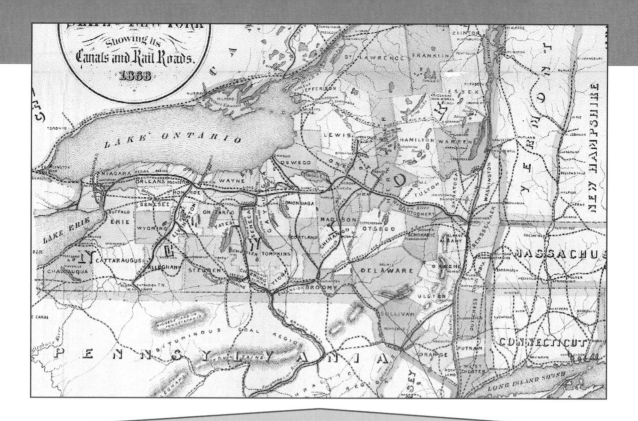

This 1868 map is typical of the many official state maps of New York that were made to accompany the annual reports filed by the state engineer and surveyor. In the upper left corner is a circle, the top of which has been cut off. The text inside the circle identifies the subject of the map: "State of New York, Showing its Canals and Rail Roads. 1868." Usually, these maps illustrate New York State, parts of surrounding states, part of Canada, Lake Ontario, and part of Lake Erie. Sometimes, the maps also illustrate the counties, as this one does. The maps either indicate the position of the canals and the railroads, or sometimes, of the railroads alone. As is visible in this map, there is always a legend in the upper left corner of the map. Many similar maps can be found on the Library of Congress's American Memory Web site.

Pennsylvania and New Jersey; and rail tracks traversed the New England states of Connecticut, Massachusetts, Vermont, and New Hampshire. Train travel was threatening the livelihood of the canals because the trains could follow routes that were beyond the reach of canals. Trains also offered a more luxurious ride than canal boats did, and they could transport goods and people more quickly than the boats could.

This double picture, taken around 1880, is called a stereograph. Photographers used a special camera with two lenses to take a stereograph. The two lenses were side by side and took pictures of the same scene from slightly different angles. When a person looks at something, the brain combines the information from the eyes' two slightly different views to enable humans to see the world in three dimensions. When a stereograph was viewed through a special device called a stereoscope, the same thing happened. Because the scene appeared in three dimensions, it was almost like being there. Stereographs were so popular that millions were made. Most of them illustrated interesting places, like the American West or cities in other countries.

Much the way the map does, the double photo (above) of the Delaware and Hudson Canal locks at Barryville, New York, starkly illustrates the competition between canals and railroads. The Delaware and Hudson Canal opened in 1828, just three years after the completion of the Erie Canal. Benjamin Wright, the chief engineer on the Erie Canal, was also the chief engineer for this canal. The Delaware and Hudson Canal transported coal from Pennsylvania to the Hudson River.

Along the bottom edge of the shot are the train tracks of the Erie Railway, which run beside the canal. This proximity of rail and water is not unusual; in many places, railroad tracks were laid right beside canals. This was because the land had already been cleared to build the canals, so it was faster and easier to build the train tracks there than to clear a new route.

The Erie Railway suffered financial problems from the time construction started in 1835. Many times it ran out of money and had to find new owners who could provide a financial boost. In spite of such problems, more and more tracks were laid, increasing the number of destinations that could be reached by train, and, ultimately, taking business away from the canals.

Meanwhile, efforts to help the Erie Canal compete with the railroads continued to be made. In 1882, New York State abolished the tolls to reduce the cost of transporting freight on the canal. Discussion also arose about enlarging the canal again, so that it could handle larger boats carrying more freight. Though most people supported this idea, not everyone was happy about it. Widening the canal would require tearing down the many businesses that had sprung up along its banks. Some people were afraid that trains were going to get all the business anyway, so there was no point in spending money to enlarge the canal. Others were afraid that the expansion would reduce the value of farmland and other property along the canal. Still others worried that there would not be enough money to finish the project.

A public meeting to discuss the proposed expansion was held in New York City on December 29, 1885. Orlando Bronson Potter was one of the speakers at the meeting. Potter was a wealthy and well-known New Yorker who owned a lot of property in New York City. From 1883 to 1885, he represented New

York in the U.S. House of Representatives. Potter favored enlarging the Erie Canal, which he strongly believed was responsible for the state's prosperity. After saying how important he believed the canal was to the state's future, Potter responded to the two main objections to the project. He argued that the railroads had not taken the place of the canals and that they never would. In his vision of the future, railroads and canals worked together to move goods and people around the country.

Potter also maintained that the canal enlargement would help farmers, not hurt them, since it would make it easier to ship agricultural products to towns and cities. At the end of his speech, Potter advised against asking the federal government to help pay for the project. He wanted the canal to remain New York's canal, a source of state pride and an example to the rest of the nation. He also warned that accepting money from the federal government would lead to higher taxes and to federal control over many state matters. Part of Potter's speech is shown on page 43.

We can see the results of the first enlargement as well as two proposals for a further enlargement in a drawing (on page 45) showing cross sections of the canal. The sketch at the top of the page is a cross section of the original canal. Immediately beneath it is the cross section after the first enlargement was finished in 1862. Below that are two choices for the proposed second enlargement. The cross section entitled "Suggested Improvement" indicates the minimum amount the canal should be enlarged. The cross section called "Recommended Enlargement" shows the preferred, greater increase in the size of the canal. The much greater size of the "recommended enlargement" indicates that some people thought the canal would have to be much larger to compete with the railroads.

IMPORTANCE OF IMPROVING AND MAIN-TAINING THE ERIE CANAL BY THE STATE OF NEW YORK WITHOUT AID FROM THE GENERAL GOVERNMENT.

ADDRESS

OF

O. B. POTTER

AT A

PUBLIC MEETING HELD IN NEW YORK CITY,

DECEMBER 29, 1885.

FELLOW-CITIZENS :

I am glad to be present with you at this meeting. It is time we commenced the work resolved upon at the Utica conference, of lengthening the locks and deepening the Erie Canal, and putting it in a thorough state of efficiency. This canal has done more for the growth, development and prosperity of the State of New York, and especially of the city of New York, since its construction, than any other agency. If kept free, and in a state of efficiency, it will continue its work of benefi-cence and blessing to our State for generations. This canal is the only reliable security which the people of this State and of this great city and of our neighboring city of Brooklyn have that the vast commerce of the Mississippi Valley and of the Great Lakes shall continue to come in in-creasing measure to the port of New York, and through it to the outside world, at rates of freight which will enable New York State and this port and city to maintain their own place in the commerce of this continent and of the world. The line of the Erie Canal, with the Great Lakes, is the natural highway of commerce from the great valley of the Mississippi to the seaboard. It was given to this State by the munificent hand of the Creator for our development and use. If we are true to ourselves, it will continue to be the great highway of commerce from East to West upon this continent in the future as it has been in the past. I know it is said that the railways have superseded, and will supersede, the canal. I deny this proposition ; and maintain that however useful and important the railways (and no man holds their agency in advancing civilization in higher estimate than I do), they by no means supersede the necessity for the maintenance of our canal. The canal developed and called into being the great commerce by which our railways are now largely sup-

Almost immediately after Orlando Bronson Potter gave his speech in New York City, it appeared in a four-page leaflet distributed around New York City and, possibly, throughout the state. This copy has Potter's signature in the upper left-hand corner of the first page, which suggests that he may have presented it to a friend.

A second drawing (on page 46) illustrates how much the canal boats had increased in size over the years and what further growth would be possible with another enlargement of the canal. The drawing shows the measurements of the boats used at different times, how many tons of freight they could carry, and how many bushels of wheat they could hold. Giving information in terms of bushels of wheat is a reminder that wheat was one of the most important cargoes transported on the canal.

Starting at the top of the drawing, we see the first boats used on the original canal. There were two increases in the size of boats used on the original canal, followed by another increase after the first enlargement was completed in 1862. The two boats at the bottom are in response to the 1890s discussion, taking place at the time the drawing was done, about enlarging the canal again. The first boat is the one that could be used if the "suggested improvement" in the canal's size was made. Below it is the boat that could be used if the greater "recommended enlargement" was made. This boat would be able to carry more than thirty times the number of tons the original boats had carried, and more than fifty times the number of bushels of wheat.

The boats used on the canal from 1817 to 1830 were 61 feet long, 7 feet wide, and 3½ feet deep. They could carry up to 30 tons of freight and had a capacity of 1,000 bushels of wheat. By 1850, boats 90 feet long and 15 feet wide were being used. They could carry 100 tons and had a capacity of 3,333 bushels. After the first enlargement was completed in 1862, the canal could handle boats 98 feet long, 17½ feet wide, and 6 feet deep. These boats could carry 240 tons and had a capacity of 8,000 bushels of wheat! The "suggested improvement" would create still larger

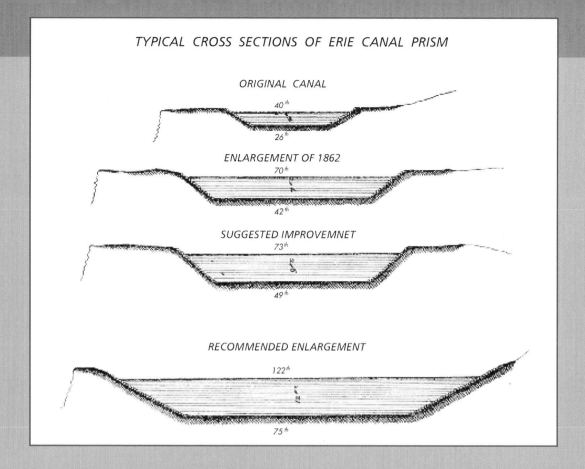

TYPICAL CROSS SECTIONS OF ERIE CANAL PRISM

ORIGINAL CANAL

ENLARGEMENT OF 1862

SUGGESTED IMPROVEMNET

RECOMMENDED ENLARGEMENT

The handwriting suggests that this drawing was done by the same person who did the drawing of canal boats on page 46. Both drawings resemble official drawings that were done for New York State around 1910 by the state engineer; those drawings are now in the state archives. The drawings shown here were probably done for the state, perhaps for the Canal Board, during the discussions in the 1890s about enlarging the canal again. The 1910 drawings have large, fancy titles and give a measurement scale. These drawings don't have either of those. Perhaps they were practice drawings done to help prepare for final, official drawings.

This drawing is clearly labeled at the top: "Typical Cross Sections of Erie Canal Prism." The word "prism" is used for the canal bed because the sides of the canal are not parallel, but slope inward (like a prism). Each cross section is labeled with the width across the top of the canal, the width of the canal bed, and the depth of the water. The original canal was 40 feet wide at the top, 26 feet wide at the bottom, and 4 feet deep. The canal enlargement that was completed in 1862 increased the width at the top of the canal to 70 feet and the width at the bottom to 42 feet. The suggested improvement would increase the width at the top to 73 feet, the width at the bottom to 49 feet, and the depth to 9 feet. The recommended enlargement would increase the width at the top to 122 feet, the width at the bottom to 75 feet, and the depth to 12 feet.

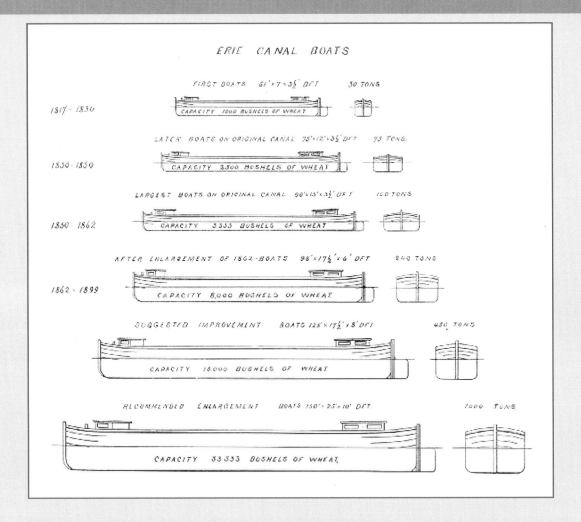

This drawing was designed to present information in a way that is easy to read. The caption at the top clearly identifies the boats as Erie Canal boats. Down the left edge of the drawing are the dates the boats were in use. Down the center of the page are drawings of side views of the boats used during each period. Each boat is identified in terms of what size was in use when: "First Boats," "Later Boats on Original Canal," "Largest Boats on Original Canal," "After Enlargement of 1862 Boats," "Suggested Improvement Boats," and "Recommended Enlargement Boats." Following that are the dimensions of the boat in feet. The first number gives the length, the second number the width, and the third number the depth of the boat. Noted in writing across the side of each boat is its capacity in terms of how many bushels of wheat it can carry. To the right of the side view is a sketch of each boat from one end. Above this is written the number of tons of freight the boat can carry. The horizontal line drawn through the views of the boats indicates how high the water will come on the boat when it is loaded.

boats: 125 feet long, 17½ feet wide, and 8 feet deep. These boats would be able to carry 450 tons and would have a capacity of 16,000 bushels. The "recommended enlargement" would result in even more impressive boats. They would be 150 feet long, 25 feet wide, and 10 feet deep. They would be able to carry 1,000 tons and would have a capacity of 33,333 bushels of wheat.

As the railroads continued to grow and take business away from the canal, the debate over enlarging the canal dragged on. Finally, in 1895, the state approved spending $9 million to enlarge the canal, and work on the project began.

CHAPTER 5

As it turned out, the people who had worried there wouldn't be enough money to finish this second enlargement of the canal were correct. In 1898, the state ran out of money for the project, and work came to a halt. Some people thought that the canal would have to be abandoned. Then, around 1900, the federal government became interested in taking over existing canal systems for defense and economic reasons. The government wanted a channel connecting the Great Lakes and the Atlantic Ocean that could handle immense battleships and freighters, allowing them to move quickly between inland waterways and the Atlantic Ocean in case of war. The canal would also benefit the national economy by allowing more freight to be transported more quickly. Even though a special report recommended that Congress improve the Erie Canal, no action was ever taken.

THE END OF AN ERA

Finally, New York's governor, Theodore Roosevelt, decided that the state should take action. In 1905, New York's citizens voted to build a new canal, and the state legislature approved borrowing money to build it. The new Erie Barge Canal would combine parts of the old canal with new routes. The barge canal would also be much wider and deeper than the old canal, enabling it to handle much larger boats. Though the new canal carried a fair

This image of the Erie Canal in Syracuse, New York, was taken by an unidentified photographer who worked for the Detroit Publishing Company, which was formed in 1895. Over the next thirty years, the company produced thousands of photographs showing landscapes, cities, famous streets and buildings, historic monuments, industry, transportation, and scenes from daily life. The photos were sold as postcards and photographic prints to people who wanted souvenirs of places they had visited or views of famous places they might never have a chance to see. This particular photograph is now located in the Library of Congress.

amount of traffic after it opened in 1918, things were not what they had once been. The peak year for traffic on the Erie Canal had been 1872. Every year after that, traffic decreased. Not only were there trains to compete with, but, later on, highways were built and cars and trucks took over—the canal age had passed.

The photograph on page 49 shows the Erie Canal as it passes through Syracuse; it was taken around 1900—the same time that the state and federal governments were deciding the canal's future. In 1820, when the canal was under construction, Syracuse was only a few wooden houses. Eighty years later, the canal's popularity had made Syracuse a prosperous city. The photo captured the clean, broad streets and impressive stone buildings bordering the canal. However, the photo also illustrates the passing of the canal era: There are no freight barges on the canal. Instead, there are only packet boats, with people waiting to board them. Once the line of boats had stretched as far as you could see in either direction. That time was gone.

Though the canal's glory days were over by the end of the nineteenth century, the barge canal continued to carry freight for many more years. Two photographs taken in Buffalo in 1943 indicate that the canal was in heavy use during World War II. The first photograph (on page 51) shows three men sitting along the side of the canal, with a fourth man standing to their right. Behind the men, a steamboat moves down the canal. Beyond the steamboat is an enormous grain elevator.

The men in the photo are helping to unload wheat from a boat that had transported it from Duluth, Minnesota, across the Great Lakes to Buffalo, New York. As in the days of the original Erie Canal, the wheat would be put on another boat, taken down the canal to the Hudson River, and then down the river to the port in New York

City. From there, much of it would be shipped overseas to help feed the soldiers fighting the war. The workers are sitting on the edge of a hatch that opens into the cargo hold of the ship. One of the workers—a scooper—holds a rope, which guides a giant shovel scooping grain from the hold.

The second photograph (on page 52) shows men inside the ship also pulling ropes to guide the giant shovel. The men seem small compared to the vast cavern of the hold. The photographer used the hold's immense size to indicate how much grain was still being transported on the canal.

Marjory Collins took this photo and the one on the previous page to illustrate that during the war, wheat and the transportation of this important crop were a vital part of the U.S. economy. Even though it was wartime, the production and transportation of wheat were not adversely affected by tightened budgets and cost cutting. Both photos are now held in the Library of Congress.

The United States and its allies won the war in 1945. The canal continued in heavy use for about another six years. After that, commercial traffic on the canal began to decline. It finally ceased in 1994.

As commercial traffic on the canal diminished, the state was promoting other uses for the canal. In 1992, the state legislature created the New York State Canal Corporation to take care of the canal. In 1996, the Canal Corporation approved a $32 million plan to improve the canal for recreational uses. They planned to fix harbors and locks along the canal so that people with private boats could use them easily and safely. They also wanted to improve the almost 300 miles of hiking and biking trails that line the canal. If many people used the canal for recreational purposes, then restaurants, hotels, and other businesses would open to serve them.

To remind people about all the interesting sights along the canal and encourage them to visit, the Canal Corporation created the colorful map shown on page 53. It shows the canal route across the state, from Buffalo on Lake Erie to Waterford on the Hudson River,

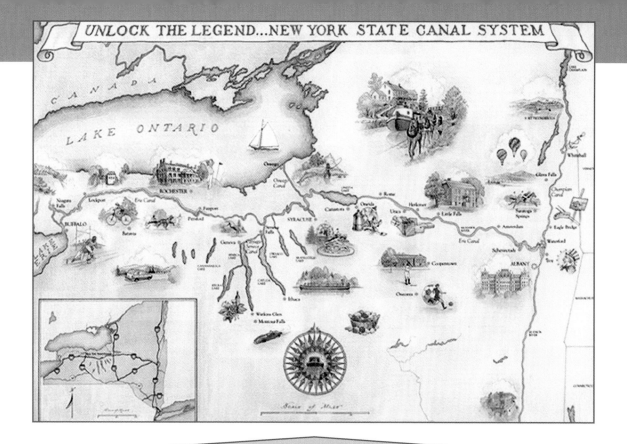

UNLOCK THE LEGEND...NEW YORK STATE CANAL SYSTEM

This map uses cheerful pastel colors to make viewers feel that a visit to the Erie Canal would be enjoyable. Spread out along the canal are scenes of the various activities one can engage in: attending a football or soccer game, riding a bike along the trail, visiting old mansions, taking a ride on a canal boat, seeing artists at work, and many other things. A small map in the lower left corner indicates where the canal is located in relation to the major highways in the state. At the bottom of the map, in the center, is a colorful compass rose—a decorative circle on a map that points to indicate which direction is north. (This compass rose points to the top.) In the center of the compass rose, at its heart, is a canal boat.

just north of Albany. Lively scenes illustrate points of interest to visit along the canal. The map also illustrates an important historical fact—that all the major cities in the state lie along the Erie Canal or the Hudson River. This is a powerful reminder of the vital role the canal played in making New York the wealthy and important state it is today.

Page 11: Grand Celebration

TRANSCRIPTION
July 4, 1817.
October 26, 1825.

At a Meeting of the Committee of Arrangements appointed by the citizens of Geneva to make suitable arrangements for the celebration of the COMPLETION of the ERIE CANAL, and the Meeting of the Waters of the Great Western Lakes and the Atlantic Ocean, on WEDNESDAY the 26th instant, it was

Resolved, That, for the purpose of demonstrating the joy which the citizens of Geneva, in common with the citizens of the State, feel at the completion of the Erie Canal, it be recommended to them to partake of a Public DINNER, at the Franklin House, on Wednesday, Oct. 26th inst. at 4 o'clock P. M.

Resolved, That it be recommended to the Citizens of Geneva to ILLUMINATE their houses on the evening of the 26th instant.

Resolved, That a Public BALL be also recommended on the evening of the day on which the first Boat departing from Buffalo, on the Erie Canal, shall arrive at New York, at such place as the Managers shall designate; and that Nicholas Ay[???], Andrew P. Tillman, Wm. V. L. Mercer, L. E. Mizner, William W. Watson, John Smith, Jun. Hiram Walbridge, James Hogert, Charles A. Williamson, Andrew Burns, David S. Hall, George Stafford, Godfrey J. Grosvenor, and John T. Wilson, be Managers of said Ball.

A NATIONAL SALUTE will be fired by a detachment from Capn. [???] Artillery Company, at twelve o'clock at noon: the bells will ring during the firing of the Salute.

The illumination to commence at the ringing of the bells, about half past 6 o'clock in the evening.

* Those citizens who wish to partake of the Dinner, are requested to leave their names at the Bookstore of J. Hogert, at the Reading Rooms, or at the Franklin House, by 10 o'clock to-morrow morning.

* Our Fellow-Citizens of the country generally, are invited to unite in the Celebration at this place.

ELNATHAN NOBLE,	ANDREW P. TILLMAN,
CHARLES BUTLER,	JOHN SMITH, Jun.
WILLIAM W. WATSON,	CASTLE SOUTHERLAND,
HIRAM WALBRIDGE,	CHARLES LEM?,
DAVID S. HALL,	Committee of Arrangements,

GENEVA, Tuesday morning, October 25, 1825.
J. Hogert?, P.

Page 29: "Table of the New Rates of Toll on the Erie Canal"

Flour was one of the products most commonly transported on the Erie Canal. The standard unit of weight for flour was the barrel, which was 196 pounds. If you wanted information about shipping a barrel of flour from Buffalo to Brockport, you would first find the town's name in the wide column toward the left. The number in the narrow column to the left of the town's name tells you that Brockport is seventy-five miles from Buffalo. The heading at the top of the column to the right of the town name tells you that this column gives the toll for a "bbl," or barrel, of flour. This column is divided into three parts: "c" stands for cents; "m" stands for mills, which are equal to one-tenth of a cent; and "f" may stand for farthings—though experts aren't certain. The toll for shipping a barrel of flour from Buffalo to Brockport was six cents, four mills, and 8.0.0 farthings. If you also wanted to know how much it would cost to ship 100 pounds of cheese, you would consult the list at the bottom of the table. That list tells you that cheese is in the group of items with a four-mill toll rate. You then find the column that applies to items with the four-mill rate (the column heading says "100 lbs. 4. m."). That column tells you that the toll for shipping 100 pounds of cheese is three cents.

Key at bottom of table:

4 Mills. On flour, salted beef and pork, bacon, butter, cheese, tallow, lard, beer and cider, pot and pearl ashes, window glass or glass ware, manufactured in this State, kelp, charcoal, broken castings, scrap iron and pig iron, stove, and all other iron castings, except machines and parts thereof, copperas and manganese, going towards tide water, sheep skins, and raw hides of domestic animals of the United States, slate and tile for roofing, and stone ware, wool, rags and junk, manilla, wheat and all other agricultural productions of the United States not particularly specified, and not being merchandize, and all articles not enumerated or excepted, passing towards tide water.
3 Mills. On foreign gypsum, household furniture, carts, wagons, sleighs, ploughs and mechanics' tools, horses, (and each horse when not weighed to be computed at 900 lbs.) and corn.
2 Mills. On bran and ship stuffs, in bulk, stone, blocks of timber for paving streets, sawed lath, of less than ten feet in length, split lath, hoop poles, hand spikes, rowing oars, broom handles, spokes, hubs, tree-nails, felloes, boat knees, plane stocks, pickets for fences, and stuff manufactured or partly manufactured for chairs or bedsteads, and hop poles, brush handles, brush backs, looking glass backs, gun stocks, plough beams and plough handles, cotton, live cattle, sheep, hogs, horns, hoofs and bones, and pressed hay and pressed broom corn.
1 Mill. On gypsum, the product of this State, (not entitled to bounty,) brick, sand, lime, clay, earth, manure and iron ore, staves and heading, transported in boats, hemp and unmanufactured tobacco going towards tide water, and potatoes.
8 Mills. Merchandize not enumerated, and all other articles not enumerated or excepted, passing from tide water.
5 Mills. Sugar, molasses, coffee, nails, spikes, iron, steel, crockery.
3 Mills. On household furniture, accompanied by and actually belonging to families emigrating, carts, wagons, sleighs, ploughs and mechanics' tools necessary for the owner's individual use, when accompanied by the owner, emigrating for the purpose of settlement.

Page 30: "A List of the Principal Places" and "A Table Showing the Toll"

The first step in using these tables is determining the distance. To find the distance between Little Falls and Rome, you locate the names of both towns in the "Names of Places" column. Rome is 123 miles from Albany; Little Falls is 88 miles. Subtract 88 from 123, and you find that it is 35 miles from Little Falls to Rome. The distance between any port along the canal and the ten major ports can be found at a glance, with no need to subtract numbers. For example, if you wanted to find the distance between Little Falls and Syracuse, you first find Little Falls in the "Names of Places" column. Then you locate the "Syracuse" heading in the group of "Distance From" columns. Go down that column to the line for Little Falls, and you find that Syracuse is 80 miles from Little Falls.

Once you've found the number of miles to be traveled on the canal, you can use that number to find the toll on the toll table. If you are shipping a barrel of flour from Little Falls to Rome, you look in the "Miles" column to find 35 miles. Then you find the column labeled "Toll on a Barrel of Flour," and go down that column to the line for 35 miles. You find that the toll will be 3 cents and 9 mills.

Page 35: Letter From Isaac N. Arnold to Abraham Lincoln

TRANSCRIPTION
Washington – June 9. 1862 –
Sir,
Should you make a communication to Congress, in regard to Enlarging locks on Erie Canal, I beg You will give the project of a Steam-boat Canal from Lake Michigan to the Missisippi the prominence its importance demands. This project is now before Congress, <u>unanimously</u> reccommendede by the following Committees
1. <u>The Committee on Military affairs</u> as a military nicessity.
2. <u>The Committee on Roads & Canals</u>.
3. Select Committee on defences of Great Lakes & Rivers –
4. It requires an excavation of only 36 miles, & improvement of Illinois River, to pass Steamers from Missisippi to the Lakes. We want Saction of the Executive.
Hon. Abraham Lincoln   Respectfully
                                                              Isaac N. Arnold

CONTEMPORARY ENGLISH TRANSLATION
Washington, D.C.
June 9, 1862
Sir,
If you are going to address Congress about enlarging the locks on the Erie Canal, I ask that you also address the project of building a steamboat canal from Lake Michigan to the Mississippi River. This is an important project that deserves to receive our full attention. It is now being considered by the Congress and has been *unanimously* recommended by the following committees:
1. *The Committee on Military Affairs*, which recommends it as a military necessity;
2. *The Committee on Roads and Canals*;
3. The Select Committee on Defenses of the Great Lakes and Rivers.
4. Also, please note that this canal would require only thirty-six miles of excavation. That excavation, along with some improvements on the Illinois River, would make it possible for steamboats to travel back and forth between the Mississippi River and the Great Lakes.
We would like to have your sanction as the executive.

To the Hon. Abraham Lincoln

                              Respectfully,
                              Isaac N. Arnold

GLOSSARY

aqueduct A bridge used to carry flowing water across a river, road, or valley. Ancient Romans built the first aqueducts.

background In paintings, whatever is behind the main figure or scene. It may be a landscape, a room, or just a solid color.

barge A broad boat with a flat bottom that is used to carry freight on rivers and canals.

barrel An official commercial unit of weight that is different for different goods. A barrel of flour holds 196 pounds.

broadside A sheet of paper printed on only one side. Broadsides are intended to be used for only a short period of time and then thrown away.

bushel A unit of measure of volume or capacity, used for dry agricultural products such as wheat. A bushel equals thirty-two quarts.

canal bed The bottom of a canal.

canal commissioner The government official responsible for regulating and maintaining canals.

canawler Someone who works on a canal.

cross section A picture of what you would see if you cut across something—like a canal, a boat, or a house—at right angles to its length, width, or height.

engineer A person with the knowledge and skills needed to design and build structures such as canals, bridges, tunnels, and tall buildings.

engraving A print made from a metal plate that has had a picture or design carved into it. Ink is rubbed into the lines, then the plate is pressed onto paper. Hundreds of copies can be printed from the plate.

grain elevator A tall building used for storing grain, such as wheat, oats, or corn.

Great Lakes A chain of five large lakes on the border between the United States and Canada.

Gulf of Mexico A part of the Atlantic Ocean that extends into land along the southern coast of the United States and the eastern coast of Mexico.

hoggee The person who drives the horses or mules that pull boats on a canal.

Hudson River A river in eastern New York State that flows south from the Adirondack Mountains into New York Harbor.

leaflet A printed, usually folded handbill or flyer, such as an advertising circular.

legend An explanatory chart or caption accompanying a map, chart, or illustration.

legislature A body of elected officials with the power to make laws for a state or country.

lithograph A print made from a stone that has had a drawing made on it with a greasy crayon. The stone is then wetted with water. Ink sticks to the drawing but not to the wet areas of the stone. Paper is then pressed against the stone. Hundreds of copies can be printed from the stone.

lock An enclosure on a canal that has gates at both ends and is used to raise and lower boats as they move from one water level to another.

Louisiana Purchase An enormous area of land between the Mississippi River and the Rocky Mountains that the United States purchased from France in 1803.

mill One-tenth of a cent.

Mississippi River A river in the central United States that flows 2,340 miles from Minnesota to the Gulf of Mexico.

New York State Canal Corporation A New York State government office created in 1992 to oversee development of the New York State Canal System for recreational use.

packet boat A canal boat for passengers that also carried some mail and cargo.

prism A shape with two parallel sides and two sides that are not parallel.

Roman Republic The period from about 510 BC to about 30 BC, when the vast territory ruled by Rome was governed by a senate and a head of state who was not a monarch.

scooper The name given to the men who worked scooping grain out of grain boats on the Erie Canal.

sitter A person who poses, or sits, to have his or her portrait painted.

steamboat A broad boat with a flat bottom that is used on canals and rivers, and is driven by steam.

steersman The person who steers a boat.

surveyor A person who surveys, or measures, land.

toll A tax paid for using something like a bridge, road, or canal.

toll collector The person who collects tolls.

ton A measure of weight equal to 2,000 pounds.

towpath The path beside a canal used by the animals pulling boats on the canal.

weekly statement A weekly report of facts and figures.

FOR MORE INFORMATION

Due to the changing nature of Internet links, the Rosen Publishing Group, Inc., has developed an online list of Web sites related to the subject of this book. This site is updated regularly. Please use this link to access the list:

http://www.rosenlinks.com/psah/erca/

FOR FURTHER READING

Doherty, Craig A., and Katherine M. Doherty. *The Erie Canal.* Woodbridge, CT: Blackbirch Press, Inc., 1997.

Larkin, F. Daniel. *New York State Canals: A Short History.* Fleischmanns, NY: Purple Mountain Press, Limited, 1998.

Lawson, Dorris Moore. *Nathan Roberts: Erie Canal Engineer.* Burlington, VT: North Country Books, Inc., 1998.

McFee, Michele A. *A Long Haul: The Story of the New York State Barge Canal.* Fleischmanns, NY: Purple Mountain Press, Limited, 1998.

Mulligan, Kate L. *Towns along the Towpath.* Washington, DC: Wakefield Press, 1997.

Murphy, Dan. *The Erie Canal: The Ditch That Opened a Nation.* Buffalo, NY: Western New York Wares Inc., 2001.

Nirgiotis, Nicholas. *Erie Canal: Gateway to the West.* New York: Franklin Watts, 1993.

Olenick, Andy, and Richard O. Reisem. *Erie Canal Legacy: Architectural Treasures of the Empire State.* Rochester, NY: Landmark Society of Western New York, 2000.

BIBLIOGRAPHY

Books

Doherty, Craig A., and Katherine M. Doherty. *The Erie Canal.* Woodbridge, CT: Blackbirch Press, Inc., 1997.

Larkin, F. Daniel, Julie C. Daniels, and Jean West, eds. *Erie Canal: New York's Gift to the Nation. A Document-Based Teacher Resource.* Peterborough, NH: Cobblestone Publishing Co.; Albany, NY: New York State Archives Partnership Trust, 2001.

Murphy, Dan. *The Erie Canal: The Ditch That Opened a Nation.* Buffalo, NY: Western New York Wares Inc., 2001.

Web Sites

Clemence, Sam, and Elizabeth Kahl. "The Erie Canal." Retrieved October 19, 2000 (http://www-fcms.syr.edu/showcase/SPClemence/ErieCnl/).

D & H Canal Historical Society. "The D & H Canal: An Engineering and Entrepreneurial Challenge." Retrieved October 19, 2001 (http:///www.canalmuseum.org/history.htm).

Library of Congress. "American Memory: Historical Collections for the National Digital Library." Retrieved October 10, 2001 (http://memory.loc.gov/ammem/).

New York State Canal Corporation. "New York State Canal System." Retrieved October 10, 2001 (http://www.canals.state.ny.us/).

Pennsylvania Historical and Museum Commission. "Pennsylvania Canals." Retrieved November 5, 2001 (http://www.phmc.state.pa.us/bah/spotlight/canals/canals2.asp?secid=31).

Sadowski, Frank E., Jr. "The Erie Canal." Retrieved September 20, 2001 (http://www.eriecanal.org/).

University of Rochester Department of History. "History of the Erie Canal." Retrieved October 18, 2001 (http://www.history.rochester.edu/canal/).

INDEX

PRIMARY SOURCE LIST

Page 9: Portrait of De Witt Clinton by unknown artist, sometime in the first quarter of the nineteenth century. This is currently housed at the Museum of the City of New York in New York City.

Page 11: Broadside titled "Grand Celebration!", 1825. This is currently housed at the New York State Archives in Albany, New York.

Page 13: The mural *Marriage of the Waters* by Charles Yardley Turner, 1905. This is currently housed at the De Witt Clinton High School in the Bronx, New York.

Page 16: Portrait of Benjamin Wright, painted sometime between 1815 and 1835 by an unknown artist. The portrait belongs to Francis Delafield Wright Jr., one of Benjamin Wright's descendants.

Page 18: Portrait of James Geddes by unknown artist, painted between 1800 and 1820. It is currently housed at the Library of Congress in Washington, D.C.

Page 20: Portrait of Nathan S. Roberts by an unknown artist, circa 1830–1840. It is currently housed at the Library of Congress in Washington, D.C.

Page 21: Woodcut of an aqueduct bridge, printed in the mid-1820s by Everard Peck.

Page 23: Painting of the Erie Canal done by John William Hill in 1829. It is currently housed at the University of Rochester Erie Canal Library in Rochester, New York.

Page 24: Engraving from 1839 of the Erie Canal based on a drawing by William H. Bartlett.

Page 27: Engraving of a two-dollar bill in canal money issued in 1841.

Page 29: Broadside, printed in 1846, of the calculations table of a toll collector. It is currently housed at the Library of Congress in Washington, D.C.

Page 30: Leaflet that contains a toll table, printed in 1846 by R. W. Roberts. It is currently housed at the Library of Congress in Washington, D.C.

Page 32: Map of the channels of the Northwest to the Atlantic seaboard by David Vaughan, 1853. It is currently housed at the Library of Congress in Washington, D.C.

Page 34: Record of quantities of agricultural products by W. D. Sunderlin, 1860. It is currently housed at the LaGuardia and Wagner Archives at the City University of New York in New York City.

Page 35: Letter from Isaac N. Arnold to Abraham Lincoln, 1862. It is currently housed at the Library of Congress in Washington, D.C.

Page 37: Broadside advertisement from 1834 for a ship sailing on the Erie Canal, housed at the Canal Society of New York State in Buffalo, New York.

Page 39: Map of New York State with canals and railroads, 1868. It is currently housed at the University of Rochester Erie Canal Library in Rochester, New York.

Page 40: Stereograph circa 1880. It is currently housed at the Mariners' Museum in Newport News, Virginia. The photographer is unknown.

Page 43: Speech given by Orlando Bronson Potter in 1885. It is currently housed at the Library of Congress in Washington, D.C.

Page 45: Drawing of cross sections of the Erie Canal by an unknown artist, circa 1900. It is currently housed at the University of Rochester in Rochester, New York.

Page 46: Drawing of canal boats by an unknown artist, circa 1900. It is currently housed at the University of Rochester in Rochester, New York.

Page 49: Photo of the Erie Canal at Salina Street in Syracuse, New York, taken by an unnamed photographer from the Detroit Publishing Company. It is currently housed at the Library of Congress in Washington, D.C.

Page 51: Photo of three men sitting alongside the Erie Canal, taken by Marjory Collins, 1943. It is currently housed at the Library of Congress in Washington, D.C.

Page 52: Photo by Marjory Collins, 1943. It is currently housed at the Library of Congress in Washington, D.C.

Page 53: Map of the Erie Canal, created by the New York State Canal Corporation. Artist and date are unknown.

About the Author

Janey Levy has a Ph.D. in art history from the University of Kansas. She has taught art history classes at several colleges and universities, published articles and essays on art history, and curated two art exhibits. Ms. Levy and her family, including two dogs, two cats, and assorted fish, live in the countryside near Buffalo, New York. She has written several books for the Rosen Publishing Group's classroom division, including *Primary Sources in Early American History*.

Photo Credits

Cover, p. 24 © Hulton/Archive/Getty Images; pp. 1, 9, 13, 23, 27, 40 © Corbis; pp. 11, 34 © New York State Archive; pp. 16, 18, 20, 29, 30 (left and right), 32, 35, 43, 49, 51, 52 © Library of Congress; pp. 21, 39, 45, 46 © University of Rochester; p. 37 © Canal Society of New York State in Buffalo, New York; p. 53 © New York State Canal Commission.

Editor

Annie Sommers

Designer

Nelson Sá